Especially for

_____

From

_____

Date

_____

Encouraging Words
for Women

Encouraging Words for Women

A Weekly Dose of God's Care and Provision

Darlene Sala

BARBOUR
PUBLISHING

Published by Barbour Publishing, Inc., P.O. Box 719, Uhrichsville, Ohio 44683, www.barbourbooks. com

Our mission is to publish and distribute inspirational products offering exceptional value and biblical encouragement to the masses.

Member of the
Evangelical Christian
Publishers Association

Printed in China.

Dedication

To the memory of my dad,
Guy P. Duffield,
whose love and enthusiasm for
the Word of God first kindled mine.

Definition

to en·cour·age: to hearten, stimulate, strengthen, spur on, assure, reassure; boost, excite, galvanize, pique, provoke, quicken, stimulate, energize, fortify, invigorate; rally, stir

Contents

Acknowledgments

Encouragement often sets off a chain reaction. Those who encourage us inspire us, in turn, to reach out to still other people with words and deeds of encouragement. That has been true of the process of writing this book.

I'm grateful for the motivation of Marcus Ryan, at www.Christianity.com, whose question, "Are you writing anything lately?" got me started. Paul Muckley, editorial director at Barbour Publishing, read the first selections and encouraged me to complete the manuscript. Ellyn Sanna, as she has done before, made sure that what I wrote communicated my intended thoughts—she is so good at that, as if she could read my mind!

My husband calls this "the book written in the middle of the night." Thank you, Harold, for putting up with my writing habits. Those cups of coffee you brought me first thing in the morning really helped make up for lost sleep.

If after women read this they are motivated to reach out to others with encouragement, the chain will continue. That is my prayer.

Introduction

"Why doesn't Alex just rely on God and let Him deal with her problems?" I asked my friend Donna. "God can help her! He's so great, so powerful, so loving!"

"But, Darlene, she doesn't know that!" replied my wise friend. And she was right. When Alex was born, her dad was so disappointed she was not the son he wanted so badly that he gave her a boy's name. Her home life was far less than supportive. She grew up struggling because she didn't know she could trust God to be true and faithful.

On the other hand, I have been extremely fortunate to have seen firsthand the faithfulness of God. I recognize the priceless legacy of having grown up in a Christian home, married a fantastic Christian man, established a Christian home, and lived long enough to see my three children have Christian homes. Because my environment immersed me in scripture, I am so blessed!

I'm also aware that many women today don't have that heritage. Although they think of themselves as Christians, deep in their hearts they don't know for sure they can rely on God. They're hoping, but they're not certain. So they're carrying around a load of stress and worry and depression that God's Word could relieve.

Sometimes when I read the Bible, I get so excited I just want to run out and find someone with whom I can share what I've discovered—because my own heart is thrilled by the jewels of truth that are there. That excitement about God has turned into this collection of "encouraging words." The ideas came from my own time in the Word, and they continue to speak strongly to my own heart. They are my efforts to share my heritage of faith with other women.

No matter what our backgrounds are, we all need an eternal perspective. We're so much "in this world" that it warps our outlook. We don't see God—or our circumstances—as they really are. Every day we need to go back to the Owner's Manual and realign our thinking with His.

When we read the Word, sometimes God puts His loving arms around us and gives us courage to keep going. Sometimes He puts up a barrier to redirect us from the way we're headed. Other times He gives us a spiritual "kick in the pants" to spur us on to do what we know we should. And sometimes He just says, "Stay here with Me for a while. I want to spend time with you." But always He encourages us, in the full meaning of that word.

I pray that God will use this book to encourage your heart. You can trust Him—He loves you!

When Your
Situation Seems
Impossible

God Is Able

What can God do? Maybe we should turn that around and ask, "What *can't* God do?" Can you think of anything?

How about that problem you're grappling with? Because you're so close to it, does it seem bigger than God? Does it cast a shadow that seems to hide God's presence? When life's troubles loom over us, we all tend to lose our sense of perspective. As we focus on our problems, God seems to fade into the background of our lives; from our faulty point of view, His presence seems tiny and insignificant. In times like these, we need to remind ourselves of the simple but incredible description the apostle Paul gives of what God can do. Paul tells us that God "is able to do immeasurably more than all we ask or imagine" (Ephesians 3:20).

In order to really grasp that verse in a practical way, I need to break it down into bite-sized truths. Paul is saying that God is able to do. . .

What I ask.

All I ask.

More than all I ask.

Immeasurably more than all I ask.

What I can imagine.

All I imagine.

More than all I imagine.

Immeasurably more than all I ask or imagine.

Wow! That should be enough for my problems today!

But there's more. Paul tells us how God can do all this. He does it "according to his power that is at work within us." That power is resurrection power—the power that raised Jesus from the dead, the power of Jesus' "indestructible life" (Hebrews 7:16)!

Maybe you're thinking, *That sounds great, but I don't know exactly how it applies to a practical approach for the problem I'm facing.* Well, think of it this way: If God could raise Jesus from the dead, is that power enough for you at the point of your neediness? I'd say so, wouldn't you? The Creator of the universe is ready to use His power in your life.

This power of God's is not merely an abstract capability He reserves for creating planets and stars and universes. He is also at work within us who are His children. Yes, His power lives inside us, working from the inside out. Our part is:

- to cooperate with what He is doing
- not to get in His way
- to let Him achieve in our lives what He wants to
- not to insist on doing things "our" way.

Then His power can bring about what we could never accomplish in our own strength.

So when you put yourself and your dilemma in the middle of this verse of Paul's, what part of your problem is too big for God?

The God of Impossible Situations

The Red Sea in front, mountains on two sides, the armies of Egypt bearing down from behind! No visible means of escape!

That's the situation where the children of Israel found themselves. Their predicament was a total surprise, for after all, Pharaoh had just let the people leave Egypt, saying, "Good riddance!" Unfortunately, after the people left, the Egyptian king had a change of heart. Suddenly Pharaoh realized he had just fired his labor force, and he wanted them back.

You probably know the story—God miraculously blew back the waters of the Red Sea so that His people could cross on dry land. Can you imagine the on-cloud-nine joy of God's people as they stood on the other shore of the Red Sea, safe from their enemies? A song of praise surged from their hearts:

I will sing to the LORD, for he is highly exalted.
The horse and its rider he has hurled into the sea.
The LORD is my strength and my song; he has become
my salvation. He is my God, and I will praise him,
my father's God, and I will exalt him.

EXODUS 15:1–2

Notice that phrase "He is my God." The God they were singing about was the God who had brought ten miraculous-though-miserable plagues on the Egyptians in order to move Pharaoh's heart to let them leave Egypt. But now He was also the God of the Red Sea crossing! They now knew this miracle-working God was their God! Israel had the God of the Impossible Situation on their side!

What kind of God do you have today? Is He the God of the impossible? An old gospel chorus, based on a song written during the building of the Panama Canal, says,

Got any rivers
    you think are uncrossable?

Got any mountains
    you can't tunnel through?
God specializes
    in things thought impossible.
And He can do
    what no other one can do.

You, too, can say, "He is my God!" If you offer Him the throne of your life, He will give you His guidance when you face the Red Sea of the Impossible Situation. He will be your God, too!

Doing the Impossible

"With my God I can scale a wall," says Psalm 18:29.

Maybe that's not a big deal for you. It does not bother my son Steve, either—he climbs the highest stone precipices in Yosemite for fun! But for me this verse pretty much represents an impossibility. I just can't climb walls, let alone granite-faced mountains. (Steve says when it comes to mountaineering, he can hardly believe he and I share the same genes!) So, too, in the circumstances of life; by myself the obstructions are too high to surmount, too difficult.

But does God ever ask me to do the impossible? I have to answer, "No." That means with God, I can get over any barrier to doing His will, right? Well, that's what the verse says.

So I'll just repeat to myself over and over, "I can scale that wall. I can scale that wall. I can scale. . ."

No, that won't work. It's not enough just to psych myself up. My only hope of getting over the wall is "with my God." I need His strong arm helping me.

God has given us some great promises, and He will help us when we are climbing walls. "My soul clings to you; your right hand upholds me," says Psalm 63:8. "Your arm is endued with power; your hand is strong" (Psalm 89:13). This one is my favorite: " 'For I am the LORD, your God, who takes hold of your right hand and says to you, Do not fear; I will help you' " (Isaiah 41:13).

It's amazing the difference it makes when someone helps you up and over an obstacle. Grasping an outreached hand is sometimes just the assistance you need. How much more help we find when we grasp God's outstretched hand!

This is no puny hand that God offers to us. Isaiah asks a question that describes how big and strong God's hand is: "Who has measured the waters in the hollow of his hand, or with the breadth of his hand marked off the heavens?" (Isaiah 40:12), and the obvious answer is "God." " 'My own hand laid the foundations of the earth, and my right hand spread out the heavens,' " says God in Isaiah 48:13.

So the next time God gives you an "impossible" job to do, reach for His powerful hand, ask for His strength, and count on Him to help you up and over the obstacles. Remember, God never asks us to do the impossible. He knows our strength is seldom great enough—but His always is!

When God Says "No"

"Teacher, we want you to do for us whatever we ask," said James and John, two of Jesus' disciples. Now, I can relate to that! I *always* want Jesus to do whatever I ask Him to do.

Their request, it turns out, was rather presumptuous: They wanted to sit on the right and left of Jesus in heaven. But the Lord didn't speak harshly to them. I can imagine Jesus slowly shaking His head as He responds gently, "You don't know what you are asking" (see Mark 10:35–38). I'm sure there are times when I don't comprehend what I'm asking, either.

Most of us understand that God answers our prayers one of three ways:

- Yes
- No
- Wait awhile

We sometimes say, "I received an answer

to prayer today!" Of course, we almost always mean that God said, "Yes" to one of our requests. But "No" is an answer to prayer, too. And thank God that as the good parent He is, God loves me enough to sometimes say "No."

Of course I always ask God for what I want, but with my limited knowledge and foresight, I don't always know what is best for me. Like a child who repeatedly begs for Skittles and Slushies, I often ask for things that aren't best for my spiritual nutrition. But if I ask for something that is not for my own good, I can be assured that God will say "No." He will not say "Yes" when He should say "No."

Did you ever notice that God the Father answered Jesus' prayer with a "No" answer? On the night when Jesus was betrayed and arrested in the Garden of Gethsemane, three times He prayed, "My Father, if it is possible, may this cup be taken from me" (Matthew 26:39). God the Father answered His Son's prayer, but His answer was "No." Because the Father said "No," you and I have salvation from our sins and will spend eternity with Him.

"We do not know what we ought to pray for," says Paul, "but the Spirit himself intercedes for us with groans that words cannot express. And he who searches our hearts knows the mind of the Spirit, because the Spirit intercedes for the saints in accordance with God's will" (Romans 8:26–27). God helps us in our ignorance and lack of wisdom.

When you're praying for something specific, be encouraged. Today God may say "Yes." Then again, He may say "Wait awhile." But if He says "No," remember that truly our heavenly Father knows best!

Facing the Facts

Once upon a time God promised two senior citizens, Abraham and Sarah, that they would have a baby—something that at their stage in life was obviously an impossibility. Now, Abraham, famous as he was as a man of great faith, was not stupid. He totally understood that 100-year-old men and 90-year-old women don't become parents. Yet Abraham faced the facts of the situation— and still trusted God. He chose to believe the promise.

Notice what the Bible says about Abraham: "Without weakening in his faith, he faced the fact that his body was as good as dead—since he was about a hundred years old —and that Sarah's womb was also dead. Yet he did not waver through unbelief regarding the promise of God, but was strengthened in his faith and gave glory to God, being fully persuaded that God had power to do what he had promised" (Romans 4:19–21). That's what I call "radical reliance" on God!

My aunt Lois recently faced a decision on whether or not to risk having a stent placed in her nearly blocked artery. Prior to performing the procedure, the doctor looked the family straight in the eyes and said, "Before I even go to scrub, I want you to know that her chances of pulling through are 1 in 1000!"

Lois and Jim had to face the fact that she was "as good as dead," to use the biblical expression. Yet, without weakening in their faith, they elected to trust God and go ahead with the process, and God saw fit to bring her through it. Obviously, God is not finished with her yet!

The facts of any situation include the hopelessness of the difficulty you face, but they also include the reality of God's power to work in your impossible situation.

Someone said,

- Look around—and be distressed,
- Look within—and be depressed,
- Look to Jesus—and be at rest.

In fact, that's the only way you can be at rest when you face an impossible situation: Look to Jesus. Focus on Him instead of on the circumstances. Fill your mind with God's Word. Concentrate your attention on His promises.

Yes, faith means that you face reality—and then make a conscious choice to believe and trust God. When we do, we practice Abraham's "radical reliance" on God.

When You're in the Dark...
and Afraid

Don't Be Afraid

When an angel appears to someone in the Bible, often the first thing the angel says is, "Do not be afraid." That's not surprising, is it? I've never had an angel appear to me, but I'm sure if one did, I would want to hear those words. It happened that way to Hagar, Gideon, Zechariah, Mary, Joseph, the shepherds in the fields, and the two Marys at the empty tomb.

Actually the phrase "Do not be afraid" is found over and over in scripture. Philip Yancey says, "The Bible contains 365 commands to 'fear not'—the most reiterated command in the Bible."[1] I think that's because God knows how prone we are to be afraid any time we meet up with something we don't understand or can't control—whether it's an angel or an ominous event in our lives.

When I looked up the phrase "Do not be afraid" in a Bible search program, I was surprised and excited to find that it is almost invariably linked with something about God—His presence, His power, His past performance, or His promise. "Do not be afraid, for I am. . ." Or "Do not be afraid, for I have. . ." Or "Do not be afraid, for I will. . ."

Apparently, the antidote to fear is the knowledge that God is with us, God is powerful, and God promises to help us.

One of my favorites of these verses is Isaiah 41:10. Over and over in my life I have been encouraged by these words:

> *So do not fear, for I am with you;*
> *do not be dismayed, for I am your God.*
> *I will strengthen you and help you;*
> *I will uphold you with my righteous right hand.*

When I was a very little girl, my dad used to take me for walks. My hands were still very tiny and his were very large; I would hold on to one of his fingers so that I wouldn't fall. But he knew that wasn't enough, for if I started to tumble, I could easily lose my grip on his finger. He used to let me hold his finger, but then he would wrap his other big fingers around my little hand so that even if I let go, he would still be holding on to me. He said that was a picture of the way God holds us with His big hand.

Yes, Lord, hold my hand tightly.
I'm holding on to You, but even more important,
I'm glad You're holding on to me—
more than ever when I am afraid!

Love and Fear

I always want to understand what is happening in my life. I can put up with a lot of discomfort and even misery if I know why.

Gideon felt that way. One day the angel of the Lord appeared to Gideon and said, " 'The LORD is with you, mighty warrior.' "

" 'But sir,' Gideon replied, 'if the LORD is with us, why has all this happened to us?' " (Judges 6:12–13).

I can relate to that! Yes, I know in my head that God has promised never to leave me or forsake me. But if all that is true—and it is—why am I going through such a hard time? As Gideon put it, "Why has all this happened to me?" When things aren't going my way and I don't understand, I begin to be anxious. Fear grips my heart.

John writes something that sounds very profound, but you have to mull it over for a while to appreciate the full meaning. He says, "Perfect love drives out fear" (1 John 4:18). My first impulse is to respond, "No,

John, I think you have it wrong. That should read, 'Perfect understanding drives out fear.' If God would just tell me why I have to deal with this nasty situation, I wouldn't be afraid." But that's not what John says. He says that perfect love drives out fear—that love is the supreme weapon against fear.

When I truly understand how much God loves me, fear leaves my heart like darkness when the sun rises. That's because love always says. . .

- I want the best for you—always.
- I have in mind your ultimate good, not just your present comfort.
- My love includes discipline, for I care too much for you to allow you to become a spoiled brat.

The best thing I can know during a difficult time is that the One who allows that difficulty is the One who loves me more than anyone else does in the whole universe. No, I may not understand the state of affairs, but I know He loves me—deeply.

And so we know and rely on the love God has for us. God is love.

1 JOHN 4:16

Shepherd, Father, King

" 'Do not be afraid, little flock, for your Father has been pleased to give you the kingdom' " (Luke 12:32). In one statement Jesus conveyed three different ways that our heavenly Father shows His concern for us:

"Little flock"
"Your Father"
"The kingdom"

Talk about mixed metaphors! Jesus used three here. Can't you just see the red circles on the paper if Jesus had submitted this passage as part of an assigned English essay?

But Jesus wanted to be as reassuring as possible. He truly wanted to spare us from fear, so He used not just one but three images to communicate to us why we should not be afraid. He wanted us to know that God is our Shepherd, our Father, our King!

Each of these metaphors conveys the message that God's understanding of the situation is far superior to ours. After all, sheep are pretty dumb creatures, children lack experience, and subjects of a kingdom don't know all there is to know about the state of affairs in the realm. But God does!

Even more comforting, each word picture tells us that God takes responsibility for us. He is a Shepherd to His flock. He is a Father to His family. And He is a King who is concerned for His subjects. We are the objects of His utmost care.

In the circumstances you are confronted with today, don't be afraid. Recognize that God is your Shepherd—your Father—your King. Pick one of those word pictures that fits your situation. Fix it firmly in your mind, and take it with you through your day. Draw a reminder in your daybook of a shepherd's crook, some stick figures of a father and child, or sketch a crown—something that will remind you of God's care for you.

Let the reality sink deep in your heart, and you will find courage to meet the challenges that you face.

Hope in the Dark

If you get up in the middle of the night and try to walk without the light, you'll find yourself groping for familiar objects; you may even become disoriented. That feeling of confusion and anxiety is a powerful word picture for times of depression, discouragement, uncertainty, and fear.

God is the One who can give me light and sustain me during these times. That's what David said: "You, O Lord, keep my lamp burning; my God turns my darkness into light" (Psalm 18:28). God brings hope in depression, direction out of confusion, light for the next step.

But how do you find light when you are in one of those dark times?

My dad, a preacher for more than seventy years, had a favorite verse in times of uncertainty: " 'I am the light of the world. Whoever follows me will never walk in darkness, but will have the light of life' " (John 8:12).

Sometimes the light God gives is only a flicker—enough to take just one step. But if we follow Him and walk in His footsteps, He will give us light for the next step—and then the next. You know how it is to follow someone in the dark. You have to stay very close to that person, or you may lose them in the darkness. It's the same with Jesus. We must keep our eyes on Him, the "light of life." If we do, we will not stumble or fall, for " 'he is like the light of morning at sunrise on a cloudless morning, like the brightness after rain' " (2 Samuel 23:4).

If you follow Him, God promises you will not walk in darkness. Just when you think you can go no farther, you will have enough light to take one more step. You will find God's direction for your life.

One day there will be no more darkness. The Book of Revelation—the book of the Bible that describes to us things we have yet to experience—tells us that in heaven "there will be no more night. They will not need the light of a lamp or the light of the sun, for the Lord God will give them light" (Revelation

22:5). We won't experience the dark of night—either literally or spiritually—for we will be with the Lord, who is light. No more depression or discouragement, no more confusion or uncertainty.

> *Until that day, "Let him who walks in the dark,*
> *who has no light, trust in the name of*
> *the LORD and rely on his God."*
>
> ISAIAH 50:10

When You
Face the Storm

I Need Help!

When you see a storm approaching in your life, one that you know is too big for you to handle, where do you turn for help? On whom or what do you rely?

The prophet Isaiah said,

> *Woe to those who go down to Egypt for help,*
> *who rely on horses, who trust in the multitude of*
> *their chariots and in the great strength of their*
> *horsemen, but do not look to the Holy One of Israel,*
> *or seek help from the LORD.*
>
> ISAIAH 31:1

In our own day, people are no different from those who lived in Isaiah's time. When people see disaster headed their way, some turn to those they think they can count on to help bail them out—friends or "contacts" (Egypt, in Isaiah's case). Others rely on material resources they can touch and see (horses). Still others rely on "numbers" (multitude of chariots). Some depend on the sheer power of their own resources (the great strength of their horsemen).

Yet God says, "Seek help from the LORD." All the time we're looking to other sources, God wants us to look to Him and call on Him for help. It's not a sign of weakness to ask God for help; it's a sign that we trust that He will come to our aid. When we call, we believe He will answer.

This is no puny, incapable God we're turning to. No way! He is the "Maker of heaven and earth" (Psalm 121:2). And, what's more, He is our Father.

In the cartoon strip "Rose Is Rose," Mom is looking up at the approaching storm clouds as she says to her little boy standing beside her, "The weather service says a big storm is headed this way! Does that frighten you, Pasquale?"

Pasquale looks at his dad looming above him and asks, "Is it bigger than DADDY?"[2]

When we are confronted with a big storm, the question is, "Is it bigger than our Father—our heavenly Father?" Hardly! Well, in that case,

Let us then approach the throne of grace with confidence, so that we may receive mercy and find grace to help us in our time of need

HEBREWS 4:16

In a big storm, we need more help than friends can give us—or money can buy—or great personal resources can provide. We need help from the Lord.

"Some trust in chariots and some in horses," says Psalm 20:7, "but we trust in the name of the LORD our God." He is bigger than any storm we will ever face.

Resting

When the circumstances of my life are the way I like them, I can easily rest in God. But that kind of resting is really resting in circumstances, not resting in God. The hard thing is to rest when the circumstances are anything but the way I'd like them to be. It's like trying to sleep in the middle of a hurricane.

Come to think about it, Jesus slept in a boat in the middle of a storm. It was on the Sea of Galilee. Matthew says that Jesus "got into the boat and his disciples followed him. Without warning, a furious storm came up on the lake, so that the waves swept over the boat. But Jesus was sleeping" (Matthew 8:23–24). I've often wondered, *How could He?* Yes, I know He was exhausted from speaking to the huge crowds and attending to their needs. But sleep in a *storm?*

I think the only reason Jesus could sleep was that He knew without a doubt that they were not going to sink. The disciples who were with Him were afraid because they didn't yet understand that the God who created the very water their boat sailed in was in the boat with them. They were just beginning to understand His full power.

Peter was one of the disciples in the boat that day. I think he learned a lesson, for years later, when Peter was arrested by King Herod and put in prison, the night before his trial, Peter slept. No doubt Herod intended to put him to death the next day, because the Bible tells us that he had just had James the brother of John killed with a sword, and when he saw that this pleased the people, he arrested Peter. Here is Peter in a prison cell the night before his trial. He's between two soldiers, bound with two chains, with sentries standing guard at the entrance—and Peter is sleeping (Acts 12:1–6).

The only way you can sleep in a storm is by realizing that God is with you. Isaiah said:

You will keep in perfect peace him whose mind is steadfast, because he trusts in you.

ISAIAH 26:3

The psalmist wrote:

I will lie down and sleep in peace, for you alone,
O LORD, make me dwell in safety.

PSALM 4:8

Where can we find rest when we don't like what we see?

Find rest, O my soul, in God alone;
my hope comes from him.

PSALM 62:5

He who sees the end from the beginning knows what He is doing.

Wonders!

I have such a short memory! When I am in the middle of a problem, I have the hardest time remembering that God got me out of the last muddle I was in. So, I forget that God is going to get me through the present circumstance, too.

The children of Israel were just like me:

They soon forgot what he had done. . . .
They forgot the God who saved them,
who had done great things in Egypt.
PSALM 106:13, 21

Yet 1 Chronicles 16:12 urges us to "Remember the wonders he [God] has done." We all have those times when God breaks through to our awareness like a bright spotlight! In my own life, here are some of those "wondrous" events:

Of course I don't remember this one, but when I was a baby, God miraculously healed me of acute mastoid infection in both ears. I should have severe hearing loss, but I don't.

When I was twelve years old, He spoke very definitely to my heart about what He wanted me to do with my life—be a minister's wife, a conviction I never doubted.

One time, when my husband and I were newlyweds, we were traveling in ministry to a distant city where my husband was to preach. We had only ten dollars left to our name. We prayed! I can still remember how glad we were to find a buffet restaurant with a sign, "Eat all you want for $1.25."

When we were packing to move to the Philippines, one morning I abruptly woke up singing the last verse to the song "God Will Take Care of You"—"No matter what may be the test, God will take care of you. 'Lean, weary one, upon my breast,' God will take care of you."

On a recent trip to Asia, I contracted a severe cold that sent me to bed instead of speaking at a seminar. After prayer, God touched my body, and beginning the next day I never missed another ministry opportunity on that trip.

Small wonders? They seemed like big

ones to me at the time.

In the stress of today, let's not forget that the God of yesterday's "wonders" is the same God who is with us today. His past provision shows us He will meet our present problems.

Take a moment to remember the wonders He has done in your life.

Is God Wise and Good?

"Whenever, therefore, you find yourselves disposed to uneasiness or murmuring at any thing that is the effect of God's providence over you, you must look upon yourself as denying either the wisdom or goodness of God." So wrote William Law, who lived from 1686 to 1761.[3]

Ouch! That hurts!

"God can't be wise and still make me go through this situation!" "God isn't good, or He wouldn't let this happen to me!" That's human logic, all right. But does it hold up against Bible truth? Is God wise? Is God good?

I'm so glad that God never gets on our case for asking, "Why?" At least nineteen times in the Book of Job you find a "Why" question. Here are some examples:

"Why have You made me your target?"

"Why should I struggle in vain?"

"Why then did You bring me out of the womb? I wish I had died before any eye saw me."

"Why do You hide Your face?"

"Why should I not be impatient?"

"Why do the wicked live on, growing old and increasing in power?"

"Why does the Almighty not set times for judgment?"

The Bible says of Job, "In all this, Job did not sin in what he said" (Job 2:10). So God must not mind when we, too, ask, "Why?"

But God doesn't always tell us the answer to our question! We don't like that, but that's how it is. That does not mean that He is not wise or that He is not good. It means simply that we don't understand because God doesn't tell us. And yet God has reasons that are far beyond our tiny bit of understanding.

I like what Fenelon wrote, a man who lived about the same time as William Law: "Let us shut our eyes, then, to that which God hides from us. Let us worship without seeing."[4] That means we must interpret what we don't understand about God in the light of what we do understand. Then we must put aside what we still don't understand—and worship God anyway.

It all comes down to one issue: Can I

trust God when I don't understand? Job said:

> *"Though he slay me, yet will I hope in him."*
> JOB 13:15

Sometimes life's storms require that kind of faith.

Strengthened— for What?

Sometimes when reading the Bible, I come on a verse that just doesn't say what I expect it to say. Colossians 1:11 is one like that, where Paul prays that God's people will be "strengthened with all power according to his glorious might so that you may. . ."

So that you may—what, Paul? I would expect the next words to be something like "so that you may accomplish great things for God." Or at least, "so that you may be victorious over the enemy." Something grand and glorious! But believe it or not, the next phrase is, "so that you may have great endurance and patience"!

That's not what I expected! True, it takes God's power and might for me to have great endurance and patience, but that's not usually my goal. I want victory, not endurance. And *patience*? I'm like the writer of Psalm 6, who asks, "How long, O LORD, how long?" (verse 3).

You've heard about the person who prayed, "Lord, I want patience—and I want it right now!" But God doesn't give us patience like a vitamin pill that we swallow once a day. Patience is the fruit of God's Spirit working in our lives, the produce that grows by God's cultivation, not ours.

> [Jesus said,] "This is to my Father's glory, that you bear much fruit, showing yourselves to be my disciples."
>
> JOHN 15:8

Patience is part of that fruit, the fruit of the Spirit (see Galatians 5:22–23).

How do we get this patience and endurance? Paul says by being "strengthened [fortified, built up, toughened] with all power according to his glorious [magnificent, wonderful, superb] might." Those are strong words.

And actually, they are very encouraging words. Just think about being strengthened by God's great power. God is the source of patience and endurance for me, and His supply is infinite. His power and mighty strength are more than enough for any storms I face.

I love the description Paul gives in Ephesians of God's "incomparably great power for us who believe. That power is like the working of his mighty strength, which he exerted in Christ when he raised him from the dead" (Ephesians 1:19–20). God's power is resurrection power! And it's for us!

He is "able to do immeasurably more than all we ask or imagine" (Ephesians 3:20). He can even make me patient!

Always Giving Thanks

"Always giving thanks to God the Father for everything, in the name of our Lord Jesus Christ," wrote Paul (Ephesians 5:20). Did he really say give thanks for "everything"? I guess, then, that means *everything*. So easy to say, so hard to do!

But Jesus gave us an example to follow, for He gave thanks in the blackest of circumstances: He gave thanks for the bread and wine that He served His disciples at their last meal before His death. These things represented His own body and blood!

"While they were eating, Jesus took bread, *gave thanks* and broke it. . .saying, 'Take and eat; this is my body.' Then he took the cup, *gave thanks* and offered it to them" (Matthew 26:26–27, emphasis added).

How could He thank the Father for His own broken body and spilled blood? The only possible way: by looking at suffering and death with eyes that saw from an eternal perspective.

Isn't it the same for you and me? The only way we can always be thankful is to look at the tough circumstances from God's perspective. No doubt that's what the phrase "giving thanks. . .in the name of our Lord Jesus Christ" means.

I think that if David, the writer of so many psalms, had lived today, he might have written a praise psalm something like this:

Praise the Lord.
Praise God in the glorious sunshine;
Praise Him in the freezing drizzle.
Praise Him as you drive to church;
Praise Him as you drive to the dentist.
Praise Him in the checkout line;
Praise Him in freeway traffic.

Praise God on the job;
Praise Him on vacation.
Praise Him on payday and
    as you make the house payment.

Praise God when you open your
    eyes in the morning;

Praise Him when you
    can't shut them at night.
Praise Him for take-out food
    and elegant dinners.
Praise Him for computers and e-mail.
Praise God when you're 13
Praise Him when you're 93.
Praise Him in the racket
    of a family gathering;
Praise Him in the quietness
    of a lonely room.
Praise God on the CD player
    and the car stereo;
Praise Him with French horn
    or drums or kazoo.
Praise Him with your heart and voice—
Or in silence.

Let everything that has breath
    praise the Lord.
Praise the Lord.

The day that lies ahead of you—or the
one you just finished—may be stormy and
overcast. But William A. Ward, a Texas

newspaper editor, once said, "God gave you a gift of 86,400 seconds today. Have you used one to say 'Thank You'?"

When You're
Fighting a Battle

Two Weapons

Picture this scenario: You're really down—flat on your face, tired, discouraged, looking up to see bottom. You feel the enemy's hot breath on your neck as he whispers:

- You'll never break that habit—as soon as you try, you'll go out and do it again.
- You'll never make it through this situation—it's hopeless.
- God doesn't care—if God really loved you, He would never have let this happen.
- God has forgotten you—you're on your own.
- You're "toast."

Yes, the enemy of your soul is firing flaming arrows at you, just when you're the weakest. And they hurt! What are you going to do?

God has given us two weapons: a shield and a sword. Paul talks about them. He says we have "weapons of righteousness in the right hand and in the left" (2 Corinthians 6:7). He tells us to "take up the shield of faith, with which you can extinguish all the flaming arrows of the evil one." Then he says to take "the sword of the Spirit, which is the word of God" (Ephesians 6:16–17).

Presuming that you are right-handed, that means you have the shield of faith in your left hand and the sword of God's Word in your right hand. One is a weapon of defense and the other a weapon of attack.

The enemy will throw flaming barbs in your direction; you can count on it. But if you have the shield of faith, you can fend off the attack, and those darts won't reach your vital spiritual organs. In turn, you can attack with the Word of God—and your enemy is no match for God.

So, the next time you are in a spiritual battle, remember you have two powerful weapons —the shield of faith and the sword, the Word of God. These "weapons we fight with are not the weapons of the world," says Paul. "On the contrary, they have divine power to demolish strongholds" (2 Corinthians 10:4).

> *The Lord is faithful, and he will strengthen and protect [me] from the evil one.*
> 2 THESSALONIANS 3:3

Claim that promise today when you go out to do battle!

The Visible
and the Invisible

Which is easier for me to trust—what I can see or what I can't see? Definitely what I can see and touch for myself! If I am sick, I want medicine. If I have a financial need, I want money. And if I am being attacked, I want someone strong to come to my assistance. But sometimes what is visible is not enough.

When Hezekiah, king of Judah, saw that Jerusalem was going to be invaded by Sennacherib, king of Assyria (2 Chronicles 32), he made all the preparations he knew to do. He produced a large number of weapons and shields. He built towers, repaired the broken sections of the city wall, and then he built another wall outside that one. Since the water supply for the city was outside the walls, he chiseled a tunnel underneath to channel the spring inside. (It still exists today.)

Hezekiah knew, however, that he must also prepare the hearts of his people. It wasn't easy to keep up their morale. All the time that Hezekiah was preparing, Sennacherib, his enemy, was taunting the people of Jerusalem, saying:

On what are you basing your confidence, that you remain in Jerusalem under siege? When Hezekiah says, "The LORD our God will save us from the hand of the king of Assyria," he is misleading you, to let you die of hunger and thirst. . . . Do you not know what I and my fathers have done to all the peoples of the other lands? Were the gods of those nations ever able to deliver their land from my hand? . . . How then can your god deliver you from my hand?

2 CHRONICLES 32:10–14

But Hezekiah came right back with stirring words to his leaders:

Do not be afraid or discouraged because of the king of Assyria and the vast army with him, for there is a greater power with us than with him. With him is only the arm of flesh, but with us is the LORD our God to help us and to fight our battles.

2 CHRONICLES 32:7–8

Without minimizing the gravity of the situation, Hezekiah urged his leaders to take into account the invisible: a greater power than that of Sennacherib—not the "arm of flesh" but the Lord their God.

And what was the outcome? The invisible God fought for His people. The Lord sent an angel who annihilated all the forces of the Assyrian king. Sennacherib had to withdraw to his own land in disgrace, and there he was killed by his own sons.

How about that problem you're facing? "Be strong and courageous," God says. Don't let the circumstances make you afraid or discouraged. A greater power is with you than the enemy you face.

With him is only the arm of flesh, but with us is the Lord our God to help us and to fight our battles.
2 Chronicles 32:8

Focus on the invisible God and take heart!

Peace

What picture comes to mind when you think of the word *peace*? I often think of Mirror Lake in Yosemite National Park. Seeing the loveliness of that spot in spring with the granite mountains and flowering trees reflected on the surface of the perfectly calm lake has stuck in my mind as the essence of peace.

But when it comes to practical day-to-day peace, I have a hard time making a connection between my life and a mirror-smooth lake that has not even a ripple on its surface. The ocean with its ever-changing winds and waves is a more likely comparison. You know what I mean—in life you never know when a storm is going to come up.

"Let the peace of Christ rule in your hearts," said the apostle Paul (Colossians 3:15). We usually think of peace as passivity—the absence of conflict. But Paul speaks of peace as active. "Let Christ's peace rule," he says. That means peace should govern, administrate, have the power over, and preside in our lives.

Christ's peace is not a passive absence of conflict but an active arbitrator in the middle of conflict. When circumstances in my life are in an uproar, I am to let Christ's peace rule or control me.

But how? Some of life's most discouraging battles are not the big dramatic ones, but the little everyday stresses we all face. . .like when your to-do list is longer than the piece of paper you're writing it on, and on top of that, relatives are arriving at your home for a visit, and you're coming down with the flu. Days like that, when you simply don't have the strength to face the daily battle of your busy schedule, how on earth do you "let Christ's peace rule"?

It seems impossible. But that's precisely when we *need* to let Christ's peace rule. At that point we say, "God, this situation is entirely out of my control. There's nothing I can do to bring order out of this chaos. Everything is a mess. Now, You take charge. I'm going to live this day one moment at a time, endeavoring to do what You want me to do. But I'm putting You in charge, not me." It's amazing the peace that can flood your heart—God's peace—as you turn over the responsibility to Him.

Christ's peace is not a denial of the circumstances but instead a commitment to the fact that He is enough for your circumstances. When we put Him in charge of our lives, the battle is already won!

Focusing on the Outcome

Just days before He was crucified, Jesus said:

> *"The hour has come for the*
> *Son of Man to be glorified."*
>
> JOHN 12:23

Glorified? That's hardly the word I would have used! Jesus was about to undergo terrible suffering! Did He know He would have thorns on His head and a lash on His back? Did He know that there would be a cross, and nails, and a spear? And what about the tremendous load of sins He would carry? When He used that word *glorify*, did He know?

Yes, He knew. He knew everything about the agony that faced Him. But He also knew that joy was ahead. He knew that three days after His crucifixion He would lay aside those burial cloths and leave that cold, dark tomb and rise from the dead. He knew that once again He would fellowship with the disciples He loved so dearly. And He knew that someday He would present to His Father those whom He had redeemed. He knew that on that glorious day "thousands upon thousands, and ten thousand times ten thousand" angels would circle the throne of God and sing:

> *"Worthy is the Lamb, who was slain,*
> *to receive power and wealth and wisdom and*
> *strength and honor and glory and praise!"*
> REVELATION 5:12

In all that He suffered, Jesus kept an amazing sense of perspective. The writer of Hebrews says that for the "joy set before him" Jesus endured the cross. He could look past the misery of the present moment to what the future outcome was going to be.

But that's the difference between Jesus and us: Jesus focused on the ultimate result rather than the painful process. Too often we get bogged down en route. The battle in which we're engaged hurts us so badly that all we can think of is stopping the pain.

We can be encouraged if we look up to someone who has succeeded in what we're trying to do—someone who has fought the battle we're fighting and won it. We have a hero to look up to, the Supreme Hero in the person of Jesus. He tells us how we can make it through the suffering that life brings. He says the secret is to keep our attention focused on our Hero, Jesus Christ. "Let us fix our eyes on Jesus," says the writer of Hebrews; "Consider him who endured such opposition from sinful men, so that you will not grow weary and lose heart" (Hebrews 12:2–3).

Are you standing at the foot of a Mount Everest–sized problem, gazing up at what you have to conquer? Or maybe you can see no farther than the mud under your feet because you don't have the courage even to look your battle in the face. Whatever fights we have to endure, I'm sure you'd agree they're pretty small compared with what Jesus faced. When your battle seems more than you can handle, look to what is ahead. Focus on Jesus and the ultimate outcome of your faith.

You can have peace and strength in the middle of suffering. But it's God's peace and God's strength—the kind that comes from doing His will and finding His resources are sufficient for whatever battle is at hand.

> *[Jesus said,] "Peace I leave with you;*
> *my peace I give you."*
> JOHN 14:27

A peace and strength that come by looking past the painful process and focusing on the future outcome.

No matter what you're struggling with, fix your eyes on Jesus—and see by faith the victorious outcome that is yet to be.

Fear and Discouragement

When God gives me a job to do, I often fight two enemies: fear and discouragement. I'm afraid to try because I might fail. When I do try, I get discouraged because the job is harder—or takes longer—than I think it should.

God's answer to fear and discouragement is the assurance of His never-failing presence.

"Have I not commanded you? Be strong and courageous," God said to Joshua. "Do not be terrified; do not be discouraged, for the LORD your God will be with you wherever you go."

JOSHUA 1:9

When God spoke these words, Moses was dead. Everyone knew God had been with Moses in a mighty way, but now Joshua had taken his place. God knew that as the new leader of His people, Joshua would experience both apprehension and depression. So God told Joshua, "No matter where you go, no matter what you experience, I will be with you. I will never leave you."

God gave a similar promise to the nation of Judah:

> *When you pass through the waters, I will*
> *be with you; and when you pass through the rivers,*
> *they will not sweep over you. When you walk*
> *through the fire, you will not be burned;*
> *the flames will not set you ablaze.*

ISAIAH 43:2

My husband often points out that God doesn't say, "If you pass through the rivers," or "if you walk through the fire." No, He says *when*; it's a given that we will have these experiences. But God does say that we will not go through these experiences alone. He will be with us. Nothing that happens, no matter how terrible it may look, will be truly, eternally disastrous, for He knows how much we can bear, and He will not let the water drown us or the fire burn us up. No matter how dark and awful the battle we face, God will bring us safely through.

When you are fearful or discouraged, what a comfort it is to have a friend who spends time with you and has words of encouragement for you! How much more reassuring to know that not merely a human friend but the almighty God Himself, who loves you so dearly, is with you in those experiences. At times you may be discouraged, and sometimes you will be afraid. In those times you may *feel* alone. But as His child you are never alone. He is always with you, and no matter how fierce the battle, He will never give up.

When You
Need Comfort

When You Need a Place to Hide

They were 110 stories tall, yet the World Trade Center Towers came down in a cloud of dust. If you had told me this would happen when I stared up at their dizzying heights a few years ago, I would have said, "Impossible!" Now, as the result of a terrorist act, they are history, and our glass bubble of security in the United States has been burst. We feel vulnerable. People in many other parts of the world have lived this way all their lives. But for most of us, it is a new experience. When the September 11 tragedy happened, I wanted to run and hide. I wanted to find some safe place where I could go to process all that had taken place.

The Bible tells us about such a hiding place. In fact, the scriptures offer us many word pictures of absolute safety: "He will hide me in the shelter of his tabernacle" (Psalm 27:5). "The eternal God is your refuge" (Deuteronomy 33:27). The Bible speaks of God, "under whose wings you have come to take refuge" (Ruth 2:12). If you want to read more, look up Psalm 143:9, 2 Samuel 22:3 and 31, Psalm 18:2, Psalm 46:1, Psalm 61:3, Psalm 91:4, and Jeremiah 17:17.

We're all painfully aware now that no tower built by human beings is strong enough to assure protection. Yet sometimes I still run to towers of my own building, thinking I will find safety there. Sometimes I run to my own "intelligent" decisions, believing that my analysis of the situation is best. Other times I run to the tower of human relationships, talking things over with a trusted friend and accepting his or her "take" on the situation rather than turning to the Lord. Other times I count on material help for protection, something that money can buy. If nothing else eases my fear, I run to the tower of my own shell—retreating from the world around me because that world seems too scary. But the Bible gives us another alternative:

*The name of the LORD is a strong tower; the
righteous run to it and are safe.*
PROVERBS 18:10

You may be thinking of the many people who lost their lives in the tragedies of
September 11, 2001. Where was God? What
kind of protection is a God who allowed so
many people to die? On that frightening day,
as I turned to scripture, I found one more
verse that changed my perspective:

*When calamity comes, the wicked are brought
down, but even in death the righteous have a refuge.*
PROVERBS 14:32

Even in death we can take refuge in
God, for through Christ, death is merely the
event that brings us to the presence of the
Father. Death is not really the end, but the
beginning of life as it should be.

Need a place to hide when life over-
whelms you? Try the strong, safe tower of
the Lord! It's a place of safety—in life or in
death.

No More Death!

Someone pointed out that every birth certificate comes with a death certificate attached. In the Bureau of Statistics, there are equal numbers of birth and death certificates for everyone. Everyone who has ever been born eventually meets the undertaker, though we prefer not to think about it.

But there is very good news! One day no more death certificates will be filled out and no more funerals conducted. Death will be defeated forever! Isaiah tells us that God "will destroy the shroud that enfolds all peoples, the sheet that covers all nations; he will swallow up death forever. The Sovereign LORD will wipe away the tears from all faces. . . . The LORD has spoken" (Isaiah 25:7–8).

No matter where you go in the world— whether it's to a little Egyptian village, a mountain hut in the Andes, the home of a wealthy family in Hong Kong, or your hometown—death brings heart-wrenching pain. It's been the same ever since life began on this earth.

But how marvelous it will be when there is no more death! God will swallow up death forever! I like that word picture. Never again will death take those we love, for death itself will be no more.

On that day God will not merely say, "Don't cry." Like a loving parent who takes his weeping child in his lap, He will wipe the tears from our faces. But when *God* wipes away tears, they will be gone forever. What a day that will be!

Isaiah says that in that day, "No one living in Zion will say, 'I am ill' " (Isaiah 33:24). You will never have to watch someone you love go through the intense pain and suffering that comes from some incurable disease. You'll never have to sit by a bedside while a dear one loses strength and life, for illness will be no more. We won't have to say good-bye anymore to those we love. We'll be reunited with friends and family who are already in the presence of the Lord because they have gone on before us.

We can't avoid the fact that an equal number of birth certificates and death certificates are issued in the world where we live. But through Christ Jesus, we are each entitled to a "born-again" certificate that has no correspondent equivalent in the world of death. Be patient for a little while longer. Death will eventually be defeated. As Isaiah said, "The LORD has spoken"!

This World Is Not My Home

We expect too much from this life here on earth. We act as if we can settle down and make our home here forever. Three times in the Bible, however, God's people are called "aliens and strangers"—and yet most of us live like we expect this present life to go on indefinitely. We work and save up for retirement as if it were heaven itself, when in reality "our citizenship is in heaven" (Philippians 3:20). "Live your lives as strangers here," said Peter (1 Peter 1:17).

We expect this broken world to hold the answers to peace and happiness. Take Christmas, for instance. We idealize the family sitting happily around a glowing Christmas tree with peace and love filling their hearts. Yet, reality is that Christmas does not always bring the closeness to family and friends that we long for. Someone is angry and refuses to come to the family get-together. A dear one is missing because of serious illness—or even death. Divorce and remarriage create problems that the wisdom of Solomon can't resolve. And when the season passes and the last string of lights is finally stowed away, we can't help but sigh, "Well, maybe next year."

"If for all practical purposes we believe that this life is our best shot at happiness, if this is as good as it gets," wrote Brent Curtis and John Eldredge, "we will live as desperate, demanding, and eventually despairing men and women. We will place on this world a burden it was never intended to bear. . . . If truth be told, most of us live as though this life is our only hope, and then we feel guilty for wanting to do exactly what Paul said he would do if that were true [Eat, drink and be merry, for tomorrow we die.]."[5]

Heaven is our real home, and perfection won't be achieved until we get there. God made us to spend eternity with Him, and although we get a foretaste here of His presence, someday we will see Him face-to-face. Now, that will be life at its best!

Job is a man who experienced life at just

about its worst. One day he reached an all-time low. His children were dead, his cattle gone, his home destroyed, his wife estranged, and his body racked with pain. You'd expect Job to be angry with God for allowing such unspeakable suffering. Yet, read what Job said:

> *"I know that my Redeemer lives, and that in the end he will stand upon the earth. And after my skin has been destroyed, yet in my flesh I will see God; I myself will see him with my own eyes —I, and not another. How my heart yearns within me!"*
> JOB 19:25–27

What kept Job going was that he had hope—not merely that things would get better in this present life, but that if they didn't, he could look forward to seeing God. Peter put it succinctly: "Set your hope fully on the grace to be given you when Jesus Christ is revealed" (1 Peter 1:13).

Curtis and Eldredge say, "Our longing for heaven whispers to us in our disappointments and screams through our agony. 'If I find in myself desires which nothing in this world can satisfy,' C. S. Lewis wrote, 'the only logical explanation is that I was made for another world.' "[6]

Yes, this world is not our home. We were made for another world. What we are experiencing in this life is not as good as it gets. So, lift up your eyes, focus on heaven, and be encouraged. The best is yet to come!

Moments of Beauty

I used to wonder why every Thanksgiving we took a picture of the family sitting around the table, for some of those pictures seemed to look very similar from year to year. It was always a bit of a challenge—you know, to get everyone seated at the same time for the picture without the food getting cold—but it was part of our Thanksgiving ritual. Now I know how important it was, for the time has come when all four of our parents are with the Lord, and our babies have grown up and now have their own babies. As the old song goes, "We have these moments to remember."

When I see breathtaking beauty or sense a poignant moment—whether it's the birth of a baby, a dazzling sunset, a stunning rose, a family gathering, or a dramatic mountain peak towering above me—strangely enough, I have ambivalent feelings. I feel awe, wonder, and joy—and at the same time I feel pain. I think it's because I know I cannot hold on to the beauty and significance I'm seeing. It's as if I want to reach out my hands and capture it and hold tight forever—but I know I can't.

No doubt this is why we've all helped Kodak become a blue-chip stock and why our continent may eventually sink under the weight of the albums and boxes of photos we all have in our closets. We want to hold on to the special moments.

I believe, though I can't really prove it from scripture, that in heaven we will no longer have ambivalent feelings when we see beauty because the beauty there will never fade. Heaven will be perfect—and so will we. Peter tells us we have "an inheritance that can never perish, spoil or fade—kept in heaven" for us (1 Peter 1:4). We'll have all eternity to appreciate what we're experiencing.

Yes, made in God's image, we can comprehend perfection now. But, living in a sinful world, we cannot achieve it or hold on to it. But we have a Savior who is perfect. That's why we find such rest and joy and peace in Him, for He is all that we long for in beauty and significance. And not only can we hold on to Him, which we can't do with the beauty on earth, but better yet, He holds on to us!

Jude says that God "is able to keep you from falling and to present you before his glorious presence without fault and with great joy" (Jude 1:24). Then he concludes:

To the only God our Savior be glory, majesty, power and authority, through Jesus Christ our Lord, before all ages, now and forevermore! Amen.

JUDE 1:25

I Will Sustain You

Our son says there are three stages to life: youth, middle age, and "My, you're looking well today!"

We smile, but in all seriousness, old age can be a frightening and needy time. In the last two years I've watched my parents go through this period in their lives. You can call it the "golden" or "sunset years" if you like, but when the days have gone far past the Bible's seventy years (Psalm 90:10) and debilitating illness keeps you from doing all the things that have brought you joy over the years, sometimes it doesn't seem like the sun is shining at all. Pain, weakness, loss of memory, failing eyesight, loss of appetite— these symptoms are not easy to deal with. As we face old age, one by one brothers, sisters, and close friends begin to disappear from the scene—and ultimately a mate is taken by death. One of my mother's dear friends once quipped, "You know, we'd better not stay around here too long ourselves or there won't be anybody left to come to our funerals!"

How good to know that God doesn't use us while we're productive and then forget us or toss us aside. We are just as valuable to Him when we reach the point that we can no longer do things for God as when we were young and strong. Our value in His sight doesn't diminish with age. Scripture says that in the body of Christ, which is made up of all believers, "those parts of the body that seem to be weaker are indispensable" (1 Corinthians 12:22).

My dad's favorite verse about these years was:

Even to your old age and gray hairs I am he, I am he who will sustain you. I have made you and I will carry you; I will sustain you and I will rescue you.

ISAIAH 46:4

He found great comfort in these promises. Never will there come a time when God will not be there for you. When God says, " 'Never will I leave you; never will I forsake you' " (Hebrews 13:5), He means just that: Never!

When Jesus was meeting with His disciples for their last meal together before His death, John says that "having loved His own who were in the world, He loved them to the end" (John 13:1 NKJV). He will love you to the end, too. As Isaiah says, He will "carry" you, "sustain" you, and "rescue" you.

That's a promise!

Together Again—Forever

"I wish all of us could live in one house," pined my grandson William when he was getting ready to leave our house and go home. "Why can't all of us live together?" To him that would be the best arrangement possible—his own family along with his grandparents, uncles and aunts, and all his cousins living together in one big house.

William, you are just a little ahead of your time. Someday we will do exactly that! Someday we will stop having to say good-bye. We'll just all move into God's big house together—forever and ever.

Farewells are so hard, especially when you're saying them to someone you love dearly who is about to leave this life and enter the eternal world. You care about that person intensely. The last thing you want is to be apart. Even when the person is a believer and you know that you will see him or her again in heaven, you are torn apart by the separation and loss.

For that very reason Paul wanted to be sure we understand what happens to those who die who have put their faith in Christ. "Brothers, we do not want you to be ignorant about those who fall asleep, or to grieve like the rest of men, who have no hope," he wrote.

Then he explained how it works: "We believe that Jesus died and rose again and so we believe that God will bring with Jesus those who have fallen asleep in him." He explains that one day "the Lord himself will come down from heaven, with a loud command, with the voice of the archangel and with the trumpet call of God, and the dead in Christ will rise first." Yes, their renewed bodies will literally rise from the graves—without the ravages of aging and disease—and be joined once more with their souls. Then those of us who are still alive when Jesus comes back "will be caught up together with them in the clouds to meet the Lord in the air."

Did you notice that word *together*? I love that word! During our lifetimes, our hearts are wrenched with pain when one by one we have to say good-bye to our loved ones—our grandparents, then parents, our spouse, and our dear friends—as death claims them. We hate death—but we can't avoid it. We want to stay together! But we can't.

The greatest family reunion ever is coming, though. That's exactly what God has planned for us. We're all going to be together again—this time with the Lord, too. "And so we will be with the Lord forever." Yes, together—forever. "Therefore," says Paul, "encourage each other with these words" (1 Thessalonians 4:13–14, 16–18)!

When You're
Under Pressure

God and My To-Do List

What do you have written on your to-do list for today? Will you get it all done? Will God feel let down if you don't?

Many of us feel God is disappointed in us if we don't accomplish all we hope. Somehow we feel that if we could just get it all done, we'd sense His smile of approval. We feel guilty when at the end of some days not even one item on the list is crossed off, because the day just didn't go like we planned. And we figure God must be pretty disappointed with us, too.

But Jesus did not come to earth to help us get more done. He came to make it possible through His life and death and resurrection for us to have a personal relationship with God. Not just "fire insurance" to keep us out of hell, but day-by-day walking and talking together.

I like that phrase "the fellowship of the

Holy Spirit" used in 2 Corinthians 13:14. God the Holy Spirit lives within us, and that means we can have fellowship with Him through His Spirit. That means we can sense His presence right where we are in the middle of our circumstances.

It's not enough to organize your life so that you get the most important things done first—unless the very first thing on your list is your relationship with God. It's not enough to learn to win friends and influence people, as good as that is, unless the number-one Friend in your life is Jesus. It's not enough to learn to think positively unless your thoughts throughout the day center on God.

God's love is neither increased nor diminished by the success or failure of your to-do list. Instead, He wants a relationship with you where every part of your life is open to Him; He wants your first concern to be how you can fellowship with Him on a closer, warmer, and more personal level, no matter how efficient and organized—or inefficient and chaotic—your life may be.

When you have that sort of relationship, you can trust your to-do list to Him. He knows better than you what you really need to accomplish.

Wait

The psalmist urges us:

> *Wait for the LORD; be strong and*
> *take heart and wait for the LORD.*
> PSALM 27:14

Over and over the Bible repeats these words: "Wait for the Lord." Wait for God to act. Wait for Him to do what no one else can do in your situation. This kind of waiting doesn't mean drumming your fingers on the table while you accuse God of being slow. Instead, it means you take courage—you take heart—because all the time you're waiting, in your heart of hearts you truly believe He will act in time.

"God is seldom early, but He is never late," says my husband. In fact, they'll probably chisel it on his tombstone someday, because he not only says it, he lives it. Yes, the God who invented time will answer before it's too late.

Evangelist Dwight L. Moody had a

brother who was an unbeliever. For forty years Moody prayed that his brother would turn to the Lord. But he never saw it happen, for Dwight L. Moody died still waiting for his brother to come to Christ. What Moody never learned on earth, however, was that after his death, his brother did come to a saving knowledge of Christ. God did answer Moody's prayers. The God who said, "Wait for the LORD" was faithful to answer.

The circumstances of your life may look like a tangled mess of threads instead of a beautiful tapestry. Put God in charge and wait for Him to act. Nothing is impossible with Him.

Hannah Whitall Smith wrote, "It is not hard. . .to trust the management of the universe, and all of the outward creation, to the Lord. Can your case then be so much more complex and difficult than these, that you need to be anxious or troubled about his management of you?"

Yes, God wants to be the manager of your life. Think about that the next time you look up into the night sky and see the heavenly bodies that God keeps going in their precise orbits. Think about it when you watch the Discovery Channel on TV and marvel at the intricacies of the cycles of life that God sustains on this earth.

If God can manage the universe with such skill and care, I suspect He can handle your life's pressures and challenges as well.

Be Still

"Rush, hurry, and hustle are the terms which best describe modern activities; but 'stand,' 'sit,' and 'wait' are words that have a prominent place in the scriptures." That observation was written by Arthur W. Pink, a Bible teacher of a previous generation. If what he says was true in his lifetime, how much more is it true in this twenty-first century, when we judge our worth at the end of the day by how many items we have checked off our to-do list?

" 'Be still, and know that I am God,' " says Psalm 46:10. Just reading those words makes me pause and take a deep breath. What would happen if I stopped a bit longer and really let that thought penetrate my life? Would it change my perspective?

I have a hard time just finding the space in my life to "be still." But I'm not alone. Amy Carmichael wrote, "I think there is no command in the whole Bible so difficult to obey and so penetrating in power, as the command to be still,"[7] and *she* also lived in a previous generation! I think that today she would say the same sentence in capital letters!

Today we use the Web instead of going to the library, we communicate by e-mail instead of writing letters, we use our cell phones to keep connected with people, we order groceries and do our Christmas shopping online. As someone noted, nowadays cleaning up after supper means gathering up the fast-food containers from the backseat of the car! Despite all our many timesaving conveniences, life seems to just get more and more hectic. Today, as never before, we need to be still.

"Be still" means "cease striving," "relax," "let go." *Let go?* That's a scary thought! It takes all the concentration I can muster to keep everything in my life in order. Yet, that's what the verse says. *Let go.*

But that's not all it says. Not just "let go," but also "know that I am God." That means I need to know that God is big enough to meet any need I may have. And He truly loves me no matter what.

Jesus sent the apostles out on a ministry trip. When they returned, they eagerly shared with Him how God had used them to minister.

Then, because so many people were coming and going that they did not even have a chance to eat, [Jesus] said to them, "Come with me by yourselves to a quiet place and get some rest."
MARK 6:31

I need that same reminder. For me being still is one of the hardest challenges in my life. I'll work for God, organize for Him, give to Him, teach for Him—usually anything but be still for Him and have deep, intimate fellowship with Him—which is what His heart longs for. God wants to be intimate with us. He wants us to take time to look deep within His heart, and He wants to speak deeply to our hearts.

If only we will be still and give Him the chance.

Good Morning!

George Mueller used to say, "It is my first business every morning to make sure that my heart is happy in God." And if you think George Mueller had no problems that made it hard for him to be happy, keep in mind that he was responsible every day for feeding ten thousand orphans who lived in the homes he established!

Whenever I read Mueller's statement, I'm fascinated. My first thought when I wake up is usually not about God, but *What do I have to do today?* Or else I'm squinting at the clock as I ask myself, *Is it really time to get up?*

One morning, though, was an exception. As I was still lying in bed the thought popped into my mind, *What do I know to be true about God today?*

Well, I knew a lot of things that are true about God—He can do anything, He never changes, He loves me, He will never leave me. . . . Once I got started, the list just seemed to go on forever.

And then it hit me: *Here I am, lying here*

thinking about all the things I have to do today, especially the things I don't want to deal with. Yet when I shift my focus to how big God is, my little to-do list looks pretty puny. I felt joy begin to bubble up inside. My heart was truly happy in God! And my attitude was different for the rest of the day.

What do *you* know to be true about God today? That just might be a good question to put on a sticky note where you'll see it first thing every morning—maybe on your bathroom mirror, or on your computer monitor, or over your kitchen sink.

Will you take the challenge? Are you willing to ask yourself that question every morning for a week? *What do I know to be true about God today?* If you find a daily answer to this question, I don't think you'll have any problem following George Mueller's example; every morning, your first business can be to make sure your heart is happy in God. The greatness of God will flood your heart.

Focusing on God puts life back into perspective!

Sleepless Nights

David had sleepless nights, so the Bible tells us. I can relate to that, especially when my life's stress level is high. It's amazing how our eyes can pop wide open at 2 a.m. Our minds work overtime in the middle of the night, or so it seems. But instead of merely tossing and turning, David prayed—a good use for those hours. In fact, an interesting study can be done on how all the writers of the psalms spent their sleepless nights. Notice these:

- Psalm 16:7 NKJV—My heart also instructs me in the night seasons.
- Psalm 22:2 NKJV—I cry. . .in the night season.
- Psalm 63:6 NKJV—I meditate on You in the night watches.
- Psalm 77:6 NKJV—I call to remembrance my song in the night.
- Psalm 119:148 NKJV—My eyes are awake through the night watches, that I may meditate on Your word.

One night David prayed, "Cause me to hear Your lovingkindness in the morning, for in You do I trust; cause me to know the way in which I should walk, for I lift up my soul to You" (Psalm 143:8 NKJV). David must have had a decision to make, for he says, "Cause me to know the way in which I should walk." He went to the right source for wisdom: "I lift up my soul to You." He turned to God, his all-knowing, all-wise heavenly Father.

Problems always look more manageable in the morning, don't they? David knew the sun would eventually rise. But he didn't just pray for morning to come quickly; he prayed that in the morning he would hear God's loving, kind voice telling him what he should do. David must not have trusted his own judgment in the middle of the night because at that hour he knew he might not make a good decision. I know how warped my perspective is at 2 a.m. In the middle of the night I'm not a good judge of either my circumstances or God's will!

At any rate, David intended to follow

whatever advice God gave him, for he ended his prayer, in verse 12, with the phrase, "For I am Your servant." He was ready to follow whatever plans God outlined for him. Maybe he'd be a tired servant, but he would be an obedient one.

May you find that same sense of peace and resolve the next time you're awake in the middle of the night!

Doing More

"God put me on earth to accomplish a certain number of things," someone wrote, "and right now I am so far behind I will never die!"

We smile at that, but if you are a person (like me!) who always feels you could be doing more than you're doing, stop for a minute. Is "more" always better?

Maybe you're thinking, *If I were just a little better organized, I could squeeze more* (there's that word again) *into my life. I could accomplish more.*

Thousands of dollars are spent on seminars every year to help people do just that—to help them maximize their lives. These training classes are often helpful. In fact, it would be hard to attend any one of them and not pick up some useful pointers that would make us more efficient.

Not surprisingly, most of us carry the same idea into our spiritual lives as well. We attend retreats and citywide gatherings. We buy books and tapes. We try new methods of Bible study and experiment with new prayer journals. All of this we do to maximize our Christian life. Sometimes it helps, and sometimes it doesn't. Sometimes we just come away saying, "Those are great ideas, but I just can't do it all. I'm 'maxed out' already."

Gail MacDonald writes, "There is a strange sort of logic that suggests that spiritual resource and renewal are found in constantly seeking new voices, attending more meetings, listening to incessant music, and gathering to exchange half thought-out opinions. How often do we fall into the trap of believing God is most pleased when we have maximized our information, our schedules, our relationships?"[8]

Maybe God doesn't care whether or not we get more done. I don't see anywhere in scripture where it says we'll get a greater reward for having done more. God does expect us to be wise with the resources He has given us, but the rewards come for faithfulness, not quantity of tasks performed.

What does God *really* want from us? Take

a look at this verse: " 'For who is he who will devote himself to be close to me?' " asks God (Jeremiah 30:21). That's the challenge—simply being close to God!

Yes, we have battles to fight and schedules to keep. But if we need something "more," it's more of God. His presence is far more necessary to our well-being than any amount of organizational skills or efficiency techniques!

Today, check up on your love relationship with the Lord. God wants us to be close to His heart—whether we get "more" done or not!

When You
Are Depressed
or Worried

Pour Out Your Heart

Have you noticed that when we pray, we have a tendency to say pretty much only nice things to God? We tend to pray pleasant, congenial, courteous prayers to God—and then gripe and complain to everyone else. I notice it when my grandchildren pray before they eat. They may have been arguing and fighting like cats and dogs as we sat down at the table. But when they fold their hands and close their eyes to pray, they talk to God in the sweetest, most angelic voices they can muster up—usually about half an octave higher than their normal voices.

Are we adults so different? If only we would pour out our hearts to Him in all honesty, until there's nothing—no circumstance, no emotion—we have not told Him about, we would come closer to what God meant prayer to be. Instead of bearing all our own burdens—or burdening someone else with them—we would learn what it means to take refuge in God.

"Trust in him at all times, O people," says David, "pour out your hearts to him, for God is our refuge" (Psalm 62:8). To trust God at all times does not mean I should "suck it up" when circumstances are bad. To the contrary, trust means I recognize He is the One to whom I can and should pour out my heart openly and freely. Real trust is honest, not stoic. Real faith believes that God is big enough to handle anything I say to Him.

This doesn't mean I should blame God for everything in life that doesn't go exactly as I think it should go. And it doesn't mean I should constantly complain to Him, not recognizing the great blessings He has showered on me. But it does mean I can be totally honest with God. After all, He knows what I'm thinking anyway.

"Pour out your heart like water in the presence of the Lord," says Lamentations 2:19. Thank God for counselors who listen to us when we need to talk to someone about our problems. But I have a feeling a lot of hours are spent in counselors' offices rather than on our knees because we have not learned to pour out our hearts to God.

Sometimes you may even need to use a notebook in your prayer time so that you can write down exactly how you feel. I have found that very helpful when I've been "stuffing" feelings in some back closet of my mind instead of externalizing them to the Lord.

God will listen as we pour out our hearts to Him. So why don't we do it more? Probably because we don't want to admit some of the thoughts and feelings that lie hidden in dark recesses of our hearts. Job said, " 'How painful are honest words!' " (Job 6:25). Pouring out our hearts to God is exactly what we need, though, for God desires "truth in the inner parts" (Psalm 51:6).

Are you feeling depressed or worried today? Pour out your heart freely to the God who is your refuge, your sanctuary, your safe haven.

God Listens!

Have you ever gone to a party when you had a serious problem on your mind? You tried to be sociable—you know, chitchat in a friendly way with the people there. But all the time you were talking, your heart was aching. The people with whom you conversed all seemed to have their lives under control. They seemed to be carefree, with no pressing problems—at least none that you could tell.

Maybe you started to share your heart just a little with someone, but the person quickly changed the subject before you had a chance to divulge what was really bothering you. She wanted to talk about herself and her interests. So you clammed up and pretended that nothing was wrong. Though you would never have done it, you wanted to cry out, "Stop! I'm hurting! Can anyone help? Or does anybody even care?"

You were surrounded with people, but you felt all alone because no one was interested in listening. If you were a man, you'd probably just stuff the problem deeper inside and act as if it didn't exist. But, being a woman, you may have cried yourself to sleep that night.

Have you given much thought to the reality that what you needed is exactly what God will do for you? The psalmist wrote:

You hear, O LORD, the desire of the afflicted;
you encourage them, and you listen to their cry.

PSALM 10:17

God listens! He doesn't interrupt when you pour out your heart to Him. He doesn't pay attention halfheartedly because He has other things on His mind. In fact, He has all the time of eternity to listen to you.

And He will encourage you! As you pour out your heart to Him, He will say to you, as He did to His disciples when He was here on earth, " 'Take courage! It is I. Don't be afraid' " (Matthew 14:27). And He's not merely an empathetic listener. You may feel better just for having verbalized your troubles, but God doesn't stop there. He says:

> *I am the L*ORD*, your God, who takes*
> *hold of your right hand and says to you,*
> *Do not fear; I will help you.*
>
> ISAIAH 41:13

Help—that's what you need!

If you bow your heart in prayer to Him right now, the God who cares for you will listen—and encourage you—and help you find a solution. He promises!

Cast and Carry

"Cast your cares on the LORD and he will sustain you," says Psalm 55:22.

That verse always challenges me. I think it's because I've always been a person who was serious about responsibility. I want to be sure I carry my end of the stick. I don't leave my work for other people to do—so it's very easy for me to get uptight about what I have to do. I tend to carry around a load of cares. But why do I carry around my cares when God says to cast them on Him?

I believe there are a number of reasons:

- I think, *This problem is my responsibility.*
- When I worry, I feel like I'm at least doing *something* about the problem.
- I think maybe I can fix this myself— and faster than God would do it.
- I really don't think He'll do anything about my concern anyway.
- It's scary to let it go.

Do any of those reasons sound familiar to you?

A verse in Hebrews, however, says:

> *Do not cast away your confidence,*
> *which has great reward.*
> HEBREWS 10:35 NKJV

God is saying here, "Don't cast away your confidence, but instead cast your cares—on Me." But what do we do instead? We get it backward, don't we? We cast away our *confidence* and carry away our *cares!*

Juan Carlos Ortiz tells about a lady who used to come to him week after week for counseling. He began to realize she was making no progress. One day he said to her, "You've come here week after week and told me *your* problems. Today you're going to sit there and listen to *my* problems." He told her his problems—church problems, personal problems, financial problems.

Then he said, "Now how do you think I cope with my problems?"

"Why," she said, "you just roll them

off on the Lord."

"Exactly!" he exclaimed. "That's what I've been trying to get *you* to do. Now get out of here and go do it!"

I can relate to that. Sometimes I need to be told that I'm taking too much responsibility on myself for life—more than God intended. He knows I'm not strong enough to carry around my cares and carry out my tasks at the same time. He knows I'll get discouraged and want to give up. So He gives me the solution:

My part: Cast my cares on Him.
His part: He will sustain me.

I think that sometimes I just need to hear those words: "Now get out of here and go do it!"

Judging God

Sometimes when worries and heartache press upon us, we are quick to judge what God does in our lives. We look at the circumstances of our lives and then decide whether what He is doing is "right," in our opinion. It's really quite presumptuous, but we do it just the same.

Where do we get our standards of what is right and what is wrong, anyway? Actually, our standards come from God Himself. We would have no concept of right and wrong if it were not for the fact that God is totally right. In reality God wrote the definition of "right" (or righteous), for it is a characteristic of His nature. It follows that being made in His image, we have a bit of an understanding of what is "right," even though we can't live up to it.

Abraham, who was known for his faith, believed God always did what was right, whether or not he understood what God was doing. When Abraham pled with God not to kill his relatives in Sodom along with the very perverse residents of that city, Abraham said to God, "Will not the Judge of all the earth do right?" (Genesis 18:25). The answer to that question is obviously "Yes," for God is absolutely just. There is no partiality with Him. "With the LORD our God there is no injustice or partiality or bribery" (2 Chronicles 19:7).

The assurance that God will do what's right is encouraging to me, because I see so much injustice in the world. I see so many wrongs I don't understand and can't change. But I can commit what I don't understand to Him, knowing that the Judge of all the earth *will* do right because it's His nature to do so.

Does that same principle apply to the events in your life personally? Will God always do what's right for you? Absolutely, when you totally commit your ways to Him.

A man once said to R. A. Torrey, "Sir, you turned your business over to God and it prospered; I turned mine over to Him and it has gone down ever since." Torrey replied, "If you turned it over to God, why are you worrying about it?"

Yes, if you turn your life over to God, you

can trust Him to do what's right—whether you understand it or not. Instead of you bearing all the responsibility, it's now God's task.

When worry and depression try to convince you otherwise, ask yourself, "Will not the Judge of all the earth do right?"

The Dimensions of God's Love

When I am in the middle of a difficult time, I may not feel loved by God. That's because my entire perspective is warped. The circumstances are so close to me that they seem to tower above God's love and block it from my vision. But that doesn't change the reality that God's love abounds all around me. It reaches far above me. It transcends time past and time to come.

The LORD is compassionate and gracious,
slow to anger, abounding in love. . . .
For as high as the heavens are above the earth,
so great is his love for those who fear him. . . .
From everlasting to everlasting the LORD's
love is with those who fear him.
PSALM 103:8, 11, 17

Look at the dimensions of God's love—"high as the heavens" and "from everlasting to everlasting"!

Anyone who ever saw Mount St. Helens in Washington before 1980 would have said it looked massive and permanent. Yet on May 18 of that year, the top 2,300 feet of the mountain disappeared within minutes. The blast area of the volcano covered an area of more than 150 square miles and sent thousands of tons of ash into the upper atmosphere. What looked so permanent was forever changed.

God tells us:

> *"Though the mountains be shaken and the hills be removed, yet my unfailing love for you will not be shaken nor my covenant of peace be removed,"* says the LORD, who has compassion on you.
> ISAIAH 54:10

Every earthquake that shakes our lives, every volcano that wreaks destruction is a reminder that while nothing in this life is everlasting, God's love for us is! Yes, everything that looks so permanent in your life may be forever changed. . .but God's love for you will never change.

We tend to judge God's love by the human love we know. When the people who should love us let us down and fail us, we fear God will do the same thing, especially when we know that at times we are pretty unlovable. But God's love isn't like human love. His love for us never fails. We need to hold on to the truth of God's Word—what God tells us about His love.

The apostle Paul prayed for believers who were going through hard times, "That you, being rooted and established in love, may have power, together with all the saints, to grasp how wide and long and high and deep is the love of Christ, and to know this love that surpasses knowledge" (Ephesians 3:17–19).

I'm not quite sure how you can know something that surpasses knowledge, but I think Paul meant that no matter how deep we probe God's love, we will never reach the end of it. We can investigate it, delve into its depths, and explore its reach. . .but we will never come to the end of God's love.

Paul wrote:

For I am convinced that neither death nor life,
neither angels nor demons, neither the present nor
the future, nor any powers, neither height nor depth,
nor anything else in all creation, will be able to
separate us from the love of God that is in
Christ Jesus our Lord.

ROMANS 8:38–39

So what does that mean in my life? It
means I can judge my circumstances by what
I know to be true about God, instead of
judging God by my circumstances. It means
I can truly rest in His love for me. I can close
my eyes, lean back, and know that though
everything I count on in life may fail, God's
love will always catch me.

*Encouragement
for Life's Tough
Challenges*

If You Forgive…

I think it's just plain scary to read:

"You have heard that it was said to the people long ago, 'Do not murder, and anyone who murders will be subject to judgment.' But I tell you that anyone who is angry with his brother will be subject to judgment. Again, anyone who says to his brother, 'Raca' [an Aramaic term of contempt], is answerable to the Sanhedrin [religious ruling body of the day]. But anyone who says, 'You fool!' will be in danger of the fire of hell."

Matthew 5:21–22

Yikes! Then, there are those two verses that follow the Lord's Prayer:

"For if you forgive men when they sin against you, your heavenly Father will also forgive you. But if you do not forgive men their sins, your Father will not forgive your sins."

Matthew 6:14–15

What's more, Jesus told a parable about

a king who had a servant who owed him a large amount of money. When the king demanded payment, the servant fell on his knees and begged for the king to be patient. In those days the debtor and his entire family could be sold into slavery to pay off the debt. But heeding the man's pleas, the king took pity on him, canceled his large debt, and let him go.

Only a short time later this same servant found a fellow servant who owed him a small amount of money. He began to choke the man, demanding that he pay the money immediately. Because the fellow servant could not, the first servant had him thrown into prison.

When the king heard about what the servant had done, he was furious and called him in. "You wicked servant," he said, "I canceled all that debt of yours because you begged me to. Shouldn't you have had mercy on your fellow servant just as I had on you?" In anger his master turned him over to the jailers to be tortured until he could pay back all he owed. Then Jesus added disturbing words:

" 'This is how my heavenly Father will treat each of you unless you forgive your brother from your heart' " (Matthew 18:23–35).

"Forgive us our debts, as we also have forgiven our debtors," we often pray rather glibly. Do we really mean we want God to forgive us to the same degree we forgive those who hurt us? Perhaps next time we ought to stop right there, in the middle of that prayer, and go make things right with the one who has offended us.

Love

What a wonderful difference love makes in our world! And it all started with God. He is the root from which all love springs. John says:

This is love: not that we loved God,
but that he loved us and sent his Son
as an atoning sacrifice for our sins.
1 JOHN 4:10

Of course, we all realize that God's love is far beyond any love we know of here on earth. Notice, though, what comparison Jesus uses to convey His love for us. I am always amazed: "As the Father has loved me, so have I loved you" (John 15:9). I can hardly conceive of the idea that Jesus loves me as God the Father loves Him! Yet it is true, for Jesus said it.

But He goes one step further, asking me to apply this same yardstick to *my* love. Jesus said:

"My command is this:
Love each other as I have loved you."
JOHN 15:12

Now, that's difficult! Ask Elizabeth Charles. She was born back in the early 1800s, yet I find that what she wrote is as true in the twenty-first century as it was during her lifetime.

It requires far more of the constraining love of Christ to love our cousins and neighbours as members of the heavenly family, than to feel the heart warm to our suffering brethren in Tuscany or Madeira [far-off places to her]. To love the whole Church is one thing; to love—that is, to delight in the graces and veil the defects—of the person who misunderstood me and opposed my plans yesterday, whose peculiar infirmities grate on my most sensitive feelings, or whose natural faults are precisely those from which my natural character most revolts, is quite another.[9]

Yes, Elizabeth, it's hard to love the one who rubs me the wrong way. Yet, that is loving with the love of God.

On one occasion in the past I knew I would have to spend some time with people who were very unhappy with me, and I dreaded it. But I couldn't avoid them. All at once God seemed to drop a thought into my heart that totally changed my attitude. *"Just because they don't love you, doesn't mean you can't love them,"* He seemed to say. *"There is nothing they can do to stop you from loving them!"*

Inside I began to laugh to myself. *That's right, there's nothing they can do to stop me from loving them!* In fact, when I did see those people, I enjoyed greeting them with a smile. I was totally free to love them whether or not they loved me.

"For Christ's love compels us," says Paul (2 Corinthians 5:14). What does His love compel you to do today? How about showing God you love Him by doing something out of the ordinary for somebody who needs encouraging—maybe even someone you don't like. That's loving as Jesus loved you.

First, Go Make Peace...

Worshipping God is a very significant occasion that nothing should interrupt, right? Not the telephone or the doorbell or anything. Yet, the Bible says:

> *"If you are offering your gift at the altar and there remember that your brother has something against you, leave your gift there in front of the altar. First go and be reconciled to your brother; then come and offer your gift."*
> MATTHEW 5:23–24

You've just started your prayer to the Lord. "Dear Father, thank You for Your greatness. I love You so much. I worship You. . . ."

"Wait just a minute," God says. "Stop right there; we have a problem." And then He speaks to your heart about that obnoxious person you had an argument with yesterday. "First, make peace with her," says God; "then come back and we'll talk." That's how significant right relationships are to God.

Now, I've seen a lot of people walk out

of a church service for various reasons. But as far as I remember, I've never seen anyone leave in the middle of a worship service to go make things right with someone who was angry with him.

Yet, when you think how much it cost God to make the relationship right between Himself and us, you get a little of God's perspective on the subject. The cross looms as a continual reminder. If He was willing to go to such a length to restore our relationship with Him, is it any surprise that He expects us to keep relationships right between us and other fellow human beings?

I'm sure you agree with the logic. But it's being obedient that's the problem. Most of us would rather do most anything than confront someone. Making things right with another person is just plain tough. We'd rather send a letter—or a gift—or ask a mutual friend to talk to the offending person for us. Yes, we probably all need a class in how to speak "the truth in love" (Ephesians 4:15).

Nevertheless, God doesn't say to wait until it's comfortable to confront. He says,

"Do it—even before you pray or worship."
So, the next time you're in church—or
on your knees—and you remember
that someone is angry with you over an
unresolved issue, "first go and be reconciled,"
says Jesus. "Then come back and talk to Me."

God does not give us the luxury of
hostility. If you don't agree, try explaining
your reasons to God.

Grumbling

Evidently God sees grumbling as a lot more serious sin than I do. Did you know that He put it in the same category as idolatry and sexual immorality (1 Corinthians 10)? That certainly gets my attention!

We don't even use the word *grumbling* much anymore—though we do plenty of it. Out of curiosity I looked it up in the dictionary: "to mutter in discontent." But look at the synonyms I found in the thesaurus: "beef, bellyache, brawl, crab, fuss, gripe, holler, squawk, whine, groan, moan; complain, kick."[10] Now, those I can identify with!

The circumstances mentioned in 1 Corinthians were this: The children of Israel were on their way from Egypt to the land God had promised them. Along the way things did not go like they expected—and they didn't hesitate to make sure Moses, their leader, knew exactly how they felt about things! They clearly had an "attitude," and as a result, most of them died in the wilderness because they did not believe and obey God. The writer, Paul, says, "Now these things occurred as examples to keep us from setting our hearts on evil things as they did." What were those "evil things"? Paul mentions four:

- Idolatry
- Sexual immorality
- Testing the Lord
- *Grumbling!*

Grumbling? I would not have put it in the same category as the other three on the list. But God does.

Among other things, God's people griped about:

- Lack of bread and meat (Exodus 16)
- Lack of water (Exodus 17:2–3)
- The difficulty of what God asked them to do (Numbers 14:27–30)
- The leaders God gave them (Numbers 16)

Paul says:

And do not grumble, as some of them did—and were killed by the destroying angel. These things happened to them as examples and were written down as warnings for us, on whom the fulfillment of the ages has come. So, if you think you are standing firm, be careful that you don't fall!

1 CORINTHIANS 10:10–12

Well, that's plain enough—an example and a warning not to gripe. I'm glad the next verse after that is one of reassurance. God will help me the next time I'm tempted to complain, for He says: "No temptation has seized you except what is common to man. And God is faithful; he will not let you be tempted beyond what you can bear. But when you are tempted, he will also provide a way out so that you can stand up under it" (verse 13).

Thank You, Lord. I'm sure I'll need that promise!

Want Ad

Not many of us file job applications with God for the position of "servant."

Actually, I don't mind being a servant so long as I can pick a time when I'm not too tired, and I want to choose the *kind* of service, and I want to schedule it when it's convenient, and I like to serve people who are grateful and appreciative and don't criticize!

Seriously, did you ever notice that serving is one of the gifts of the Spirit—though, I must add, it's not one of the more popular ones. The Book of Romans says:

> *We have different gifts, according to the grace given us. If a man's gift is. . .serving, let him serve.*
> ROMANS 12:6–7

Even though we're told to "eagerly desire spiritual gifts" (1 Corinthians 14:1), I've never personally known anyone who prayed that God would give him the gift of serving. Yet every spiritual gift in reality is a gift of service, for Peter says:

*Each one should use whatever gift he has
received to serve others, faithfully administering
God's grace in its various forms.*
1 PETER 4:10

Whoever wants to become great must be a servant, Jesus said—" 'just as the Son of Man did not come to be served, but to serve, and to give his life as a ransom for many' " (Matthew 20:28). One thing is for sure: We can never say that Jesus asks us to do something He was not willing to do. He spent His entire lifetime serving others. We could list many examples, but the one that always sticks in my mind is the instance when He washed the disciples' feet—a mundane, messy, stinky job—shortly before His crucifixion. What an example!

What would happen in this world if we all truly began to serve one another? We'd hear more phrases like, "What can I do to help?" "No, don't get up—let me get that for you." "You're so tired—why don't you lie down and let me clean up the mess?"

Some friends of ours decided that in their family, beginning with the dad clear down to the youngest, they would begin serving one another. Sometimes it was humorous as they nearly stumbled over each other trying to be helpful. But I will say that the whole atmosphere of their home changed with that attitude.

In this Me Generation, positions are going unfilled for the job of "servant." Want to apply? What a difference it would make in our weary world if we would only "serve one another in love" (Galatians 5:13)!

What Shall
I Wear Today?

Every morning you go to the closet and decide what you're going to wear. It's one of the first decisions of the day. Will it be jeans or dress clothes? Black or brown? Cotton, wool—or microfiber? If you're the parent of small kids, you choose clothes for them to wear even though you know you'll probably hear them say, "I don't want to wear *that*!" When one of our daughters was in high school, she actually kept a diary of what she wore to school each day so that she wouldn't duplicate her outfits too often! I used to wonder how her friends would possibly remember what she wore if *she* couldn't.

Did you know that God has a clothes closet and that you can make selections of what you're going to wear from His wardrobe?

As God's chosen people, holy and dearly loved,
clothe yourselves with. . .
COLOSSIANS 3:12

Paul goes on to list five wardrobe selections: compassion, kindness, humility, gentleness, and patience.

"I don't think I want to put on patience today—at least not until I have a chance to give my husband a piece of my mind about how he talked to me yesterday! Humility? No, I'm a bit too big for humility to fit now. Gentleness doesn't quite suit me, either. Kindness? That's something I wish my kids would wear! They're always arguing over who gets what!"

The fact that Paul says we can "put on" these qualities must mean we have a choice. I have something to do with whether or not these qualities are evident in my life. That means it's pretty important that I get up in the morning in time to get "dressed" spiritually from God's wardrobe before I face my day.

But individual pieces of clothing don't necessarily make an outfit. Often it takes one special piece that pulls the whole thing together. Verse 14 tells us what that garment is in God's wardrobe:

Over all these virtues put on love,
which binds them all together in perfect unity.
COLOSSIANS 3:14

Love is the garment that coordinates and pulls the outfit all together. Love makes me truly "pleasing to the eye."

Wouldn't we all be a lot more attractive if we dressed in God's wardrobe?

Level Paths for
Your Feet

I've been fascinated by that little phrase
in the Bible: "Make level paths for your feet"
(Hebrews 12:13). In this chapter of Hebrews,
the Christian life is compared to running a
race on a course that is laid out. But how do I
make the path level?

I make a level path when I do all in my
power to set up the circumstances in such
a way that it's easy to do right and hard to
do wrong. I just did that recently. Because
of some early heart problems, my husband
chose to stop eating fatty foods, and I
decided to do the same. I thought of this
phrase, "Make level paths for your feet,"
when I cleared out the pantry of foods we
had decided we would no longer eat. The big
change in eating was much easier that way.
Okay, that's not a very "spiritual" example,
but that verse helped me just the same.

I'm also making level paths for my feet
when I make sure I'm on the right path to

begin with. King David got himself in deep trouble by not being on the right track. He wasn't where he should be.

> *In the spring, at the time when kings go off to war, David sent Joab out with the king's men and the whole Israelite army. . . . But David remained in Jerusalem.*
>
> 2 SAMUEL 11:1

And he got tripped up on the path he chose.

Yes, David should have been out there with his men, and because of that wrong choice, we learn in the very next verse that he immediately got in trouble: "One evening David got up from his bed and walked around on the roof of the palace. From the roof he saw a woman bathing. The woman was very beautiful. . . ." And it was all downhill from there. David committed adultery with Bathsheba, got her pregnant, and then had her husband killed to try to cover up what he had done. None of it would ever have happened if David had been on the right track to start with.

But let's assume you have chosen the right course. What else can you do to make level paths for your feet? For one thing, keep your map—God's Word—where you can easily read and absorb it. My friend Marta kept two Bibles open in her home. The one upstairs was open to the Old Testament, and the one downstairs was open to the New Testament. Every time she passed by, she found it easy to "grab" a few verses to think about. You probably own several Bibles. Where do you keep them? Are they readily available?

You can decide ahead of time how you are going to live your life. You can decide what kind of movies and TV shows you're going to watch, what type of books and magazines you're going to have in your home—even what kind of thoughts you're going to dwell on in your mind. You simplify your life a great deal if you make these decisions ahead of time, drawing a line and saying, "This is how I'm going to live, and that's settled!"

Yes, there are bound to be bumps along

the way, but with God's help you can "throw off everything that hinders and the sin that so easily entangles" and "run with perseverance the race marked out" for you (Hebrews 12:1)—on a level path.

*Encouragement
for Ordinary Days*

How to Be Perfect—
Well, Nearly!

Do you know someone who is really godly? I think I can tell you something about that person even without meeting him or her: That person probably has the ability to say the right things at the right time. I don't mean the person is "perfect," but she no doubt knows when to keep her mouth shut and when to speak up. She knows how to bless people with her words. That's because if a person's tongue is disciplined, the rest of her life will follow.

James told us:

We all stumble in many ways. If anyone is never at fault in what he says, he is a perfect man, able to keep his whole body in check.

JAMES 3:2

For some of us, that means keeping our mouths shut more often. After all, a closed mouth gathers no foot! But nobody said it's easy. Solomon said:

> *When words are many, sin is not absent,*
> *but he who holds his tongue is wise.*
> PROVERBS 10:19

James further added:

> *If anyone considers himself religious and yet does*
> *not keep a tight rein on his tongue, he deceives*
> *himself and his religion is worthless.*
> JAMES 1:26

If we're not talking, that means we're probably listening, and really listening is one of the hardest things to do! A number of years ago, I decided to do an experiment in listening. The rules I set for myself were, "For a whole week when I talk to people, I will not offer any advice. I will just listen. I will draw out the other person but keep my mouth shut when it comes to telling them what to do." If you don't think that was difficult, just try it! I was amazed how much hard work it was to listen. More revealing was how often I felt compelled to add my two cents' worth. If biting my tongue required adhesive bandages, mine would have been well swathed!

James gives us one more bit of advice:

> *My dear brothers, take note of this:*
> *Everyone should be quick to listen,*
> *slow to speak and slow to become angry.*
>
> JAMES 1:19

How often anger triggers hurtful words! Let anger be a red flag—a warning to follow through with Spirit-control.

"Godly" is not something we simply decide to be. It's the description of a person who truly follows Jesus so closely that she becomes like Him. But you can be sure when you meet that person, he or she will be someone whose tongue brings blessing and whose words draw you to the Lord.

I Keep Forgetting. . . .

Do you have the same problem I have? You read your Bible—and thirty minutes later you can't remember what you've read? It's frustrating! Why does it happen? What keeps us from remembering?

Three things, says Jesus in Mark 4:19. See if it isn't true in your life.

- *The worries of this life.* Life's uncertainties center your attention on your problems instead of on God, and you forget that He said, "Do not worry about tomorrow" (Matthew 6:34). When I'm in the middle of a mess, I have tunnel vision that focuses on my problem. Encouraging Bible verses just don't flood my mind automatically. I have to discipline my thoughts to concentrate on the truths of God's Word. The "worries of this life" literally choke out the seed.

When I sit down to read the Bible, I think the devil delights in taking those moments to remind me of the jillion things I need to do that day. I'm learning that it's helpful to have a notebook nearby so I can jot down those things—and then get back to focusing on the Lord.

- *The deceitfulness of wealth.* The false security of money makes us think if we have enough dollars in our wallet, we won't need God. Some of us may not have enough money and so our thoughts are full of financial worries—while others of us have all the money we could ever need and yet we can't stop thinking about our bank accounts. Either way, we are falling for the lie that says money can offer us true happiness; we are allowing financial concerns to distract our focus from God. He is the One who will supply our deepest, truest needs—not money.

- *The desires for other things.* Always wanting more "things" makes God's Word seem less significant by comparison. Because we're focused on what we want from God, we don't see what He wants from us. When you stop and think about it, probably the worst thing we can do to God is to want *something* more than we want Him. When that happens, we've begun worshipping an idol instead of the Creator who loves us.

How do we combat this tendency to forget the encouragement we find in scripture? First, prepare the soil of your heart to receive the seed of God's Word. Ask God to break up the hard surface and root out any stones that would keep the seed from growing. Then, I find it helps to write down the truth He shows me. I have a friend who writes a letter to God every day. The letter is really a prayer that contains all the concerns of her heart and the truths that God has spoken to her. When she is finished, she throws the letter away, because it is very personal. But writing the letter helps her to focus—and to remember. Not a bad idea!

And most importantly, we can ask the Holy Spirit to help us remember. That's His job, you know. Just before Jesus died, He said:

"But the Counselor, the Holy Spirit, whom the Father will send in my name, will teach you all things and will remind you of everything I have said to you."
JOHN 14:26

Come, Holy Spirit, I need You!

A Reason to Get Rich?

A beautiful glossy black Mercedes was in the lane next to us on the freeway. As we got closer, I noticed the license plate: "MT 633." I figured that must be a Bible verse. I couldn't help smiling as I recalled what Matthew 6:33 says:

> But seek first his kingdom and his righteousness, and all these things will be given to you as well.

Translation: "Put God first, and you can drive one of these, too!"

While that rendition may make following Jesus very popular, somehow I don't think that's exactly what He meant when He made that statement. Most of the people He was talking to that day on the hillside of Galilee were anxious about not having enough money for the meager basics of food and clothing.

It's not wrong to be rich. It's just a lot of responsibility. Frank Lloyd Wright, the famous architect who was well-off himself, once said, "Many wealthy people are little more than janitors of their possessions." I think that's what Jesus was trying to spare us from when He said, "Do not store up for yourselves treasures on earth, where moth and rust destroy, and where thieves break in and steal. But store up for yourselves treasures in heaven" (Matthew 6:19–20).

There are only four things you can do with money: hoard it, waste it, invest it, or spend it, which includes of course giving it away. The Bible says:

Whoever sows sparingly will also reap sparingly, and whoever sows generously will also reap generously.
2 Corinthians 9:6

That leads some people to say, "Then, give in order to get rich! The more you give to God, the more He will give back to you."

If you give to God, it is true that He will bless you, for He always pours out a cascade of blessings on us compared with the little cupful we give to Him. But is that the right motive for giving? No, the idea of giving in order to get more and more "goodies" for us just isn't a Bible idea.

God wants us to use wealth (and compared to most of the world, we are nearly all wealthy!) to help other people, not ourselves. Take a look at these verses (emphasis added):

- "You will be made rich in every way *so that you can be generous* on every occasion" (2 Corinthians 9:11).
- God makes His grace "abound" to us so that we will "*abound in every good work*" (2 Corinthians 9:8).
- "He who has been stealing must steal no longer, but must work. . .*that he may have something to share* with those in need" (Ephesians 4:28).

Do you see a pattern in those verses? Not "give in order to *get*," but "get in order to *give*." Pretty clear, isn't it?

Heat or Drought?

Are you in the middle of a battle zone right now with the bullets flying everywhere? Or is this a dry period in your life when absolutely nothing seems to be happening? In life we experience both kinds of situations.

The Bible says God is sufficient for both—for intense problems and for total barrenness.

> *"Blessed is the man who trusts in the LORD, whose confidence is in him. He will be like a tree planted by the water. . . . It does not fear when heat comes. . . . It has no worries in a year of drought."*
>
> JEREMIAH 17:7–8

There it is—two different types of circumstances: heat and drought.

Heat speaks of intense trials. During those times you struggle as you are attacked with problems that come at you, one after another. You wonder if life will ever settle down again. No sooner do you catch your breath from one crisis than another hits you.

On the other hand, drought symbolizes those dry times when you feel like nothing—not anything, zero, nil, zilch—is taking place in your life. And no one seems to care. Either way, if the roots of your confidence go deep into God, you will find that He is sufficient.

Where is your confidence and trust? Be honest. Is it in yourself? In fate? Or in God? Do your roots go down deep enough to draw from the River of Life? Or are you just hoping for a few sprinkles from heaven? Jesus said, " 'To him who is thirsty I will give to drink without cost from the spring of the water of life' " (Revelation 21:6).

Right now, whether you are experiencing severe heat or the barrenness of drought, drink deeply of the water of life that really satisfies. Don't live in a state of spiritual dehydration. Let your roots go down into the resources of God. Paul summed it up by urging,

So then, just as you received Christ Jesus as Lord,
continue to live in him, rooted and built up in him,
strengthened in the faith.
COLOSSIANS 2:6–7

So, don't give up. The Water of Life still flows to refresh you and strengthen you. Remember that God says, "Blessed is the man who trusts in the LORD, whose confidence is in him. He will be like a tree planted by the water." Rooted in Him, we have all that we need to withstand both heat and drought.

For His Own Sake

God blots out my sins and forgets them forever! That's what the Bible tells me:

"I, even I, am he who blots out your transgressions, for my own sake, and remembers your sins no more."
ISAIAH 43:25

I'm so thankful He removes my sins with His divine eraser, and I'm even more thankful that He never remembers them again.

But only recently did I really notice the part of that verse that says God blots out my sins for His own sake. I always thought God came up with the plan to provide for my sins to be wiped out for *my* sake—that He so loved the world that He gave His Son to pay for my sins so that I could have eternal life. But this verse says He did it for *His* sake.

Does this mean God wanted my fellowship so much that He was willing to send Jesus to die on the cross to make that fellowship possible? Incredible! God paid that unbelievably high price to do away with my sins—for *His* sake! He wants a relationship with me that was not possible except at great cost to God!

It follows, then, that communication with God—what we call "prayer"—must be very important to this great One who wants fellowship with me so much. That changes the whole concept of prayer. Yes, God gives me what I need when I ask Him, but He doesn't want me to wait to communicate with Him until I have a problem. He wants me to talk to Him simply because He loves to hear my voice!

As a mother tucked her little boy in bed one night, she asked him if he had said his prayers. "No, Mom," he replied, "I don't need anything tonight." So often I'm like that little boy. Prayer is not just bringing my grocery list of needs to God. He wants to walk with me and talk with me all the time. He wants fellowship with *me*. To make this possible, He wiped out my sins—for His own sake! Yes, He really wants close friendship with me. What a marvelous reality!

We don't only talk to our friends or

spouses when we need something from them. We talk for the pure joy of talking. So why should we wait to pray until we need something? God doesn't need anything, either—but He wants to talk with us and have companionship with us.

God Notices!

God notices everything! He really does. He sees you on a steaming July day when you take an ice-cold soda out to the guy who is pulling weeds in your backyard. He knows when you bite your tongue instead of yelling at your son because of the spilled orange juice when he insisted on "helping" you fix breakfast. He saw that understanding hug you gave your husband after the garage post reached out and bent his car fender. Yes, He sees.

And someday He will reward you. "Wait till the Lord comes," the apostle Paul writes. "He will bring to light what is hidden in darkness and will expose the motives of men's hearts. At that time each will receive his praise from God" (1 Corinthians 4:5).

Sometimes we're quick to do kind things when people are watching and not so quick when we think no one will ever see. But the true test of faithfulness to God is our willingness to do what pleases Him day after day after day when no one else knows.

A pastor's wife and personal friend of
my parents, Ruth Harms Calkin, wrote this
prayer called "I Wonder":

You know, Lord,
How I serve You
With great emotional fervor
In the limelight.
You know how eagerly
I speak for You
At a women's club.
You know how I effervesce
When I promote
A fellowship group.
You know my genuine enthusiasm
At a Bible study.
But how would I react, I wonder,
If You pointed to a basin of water
And asked me to wash
The calloused feet
Of a bent and wrinkled old woman
Day after day,
Month after month,
In a room where nobody saw
And nobody knew?[11]

"Love's secret is to be always doing things for God," wrote F. W. Faber back in the 1800s, and then he added, "and not to mind because they are such very little ones."

You may never receive recognition in this life for the kind things you do, but someday you will receive praise from God. He notices!

Running the Race

I've always liked the way the Bible compares life to a race. "Let us run with perseverance the race marked out for us," says the author of Hebrews 12:1. But in comparing life to a race, don't be confused and think that everybody is in one enormous contest—a single race for all of us. Did you notice that phrase "the race marked out for us"? God has a race for you that is unique. Yours may be a 100-yard dash while someone else runs 1500 meters, still another runs a 10-K or a marathon, and for yet others life's race seems to be hurdles—they hardly make it over one obstacle before another rises in front of them.

We're not in competition with one another. That's why we shouldn't look at the person next to us and think, *She's not running as fast as I am.* Or, *He's making terrific progress in his life, while I'm going nowhere right now.*

Let me encourage you with this thought: You can run the race God has set out for you because it's designed uniquely for you.

It's neither too long nor too difficult for you. God knows your strengths and your weaknesses, your abilities and inabilities, and He takes these into account as He lays out the course. You'll be stretched more than you ever thought you could endure, but He'll never ask you to do the impossible. He has promised His presence and His resources as you call on Him for what you need.

Sometimes dark times discourage us—but they can also give us new determination to make our lives count as never before. In response to the tragedy of September 11, 2001, a friend of mine wrote, "I feel I am facing a deeper challenge to be all that I can be, to reach out in as many ways as I can as far as I can, to use whatever gifts God has given me with all my heart."

As you seek encouragement in your life, perhaps God is also speaking to you about your need for renewed purpose in the race you are running. Perhaps as you read Hebrews 12:1 the word *perseverance* stood out in bold letters. Have you been slacking off lately or getting sidetracked by discouragement? The secret is found in Hebrews 12:2: "Let us fix our eyes on Jesus, the author and perfecter of our faith." It's only when we take our eyes off Him that we get off track. As we keep our focus on Jesus, we progress ever closer to Him, our source of faith, purpose, courage, and direction.

Embrace the race you are running as designed for you by God Himself. Accept the opportunities and obstacles that are before you as part of His plan. Set your sights on Jesus. Then once more take a deep breath and get going.

For additional help,
write to Darlene Sala:

In the United States—
c/o Guidelines International Ministries
Box G
Laguna Hills, CA 92654

In Asia—
c/o Guidelines International Ministries
P.O. Box 4000
Makati City, MM, Philippines

Endnotes

1. Philip Yancey, *Reaching for the Invisible God* (Grand Rapids, MI: Zondervan, 2000), p. 81.

2. Pat Brady, "Rose Is Rose," *Orange County Register*, Accent Section (30 July 1993), p. 4.

3. Quoted in Mary W. Tileston, *Daily Strength for Daily Needs* (Uhrichsville, OH: Barbour, 1990), p. 287.

4. Ibid., p. 285.

5. Brent Curtis and John Eldredge, *The Sacred Romance* (Nashville, TN: Thomas Nelson, 1997), pp. 179–180.

6. Ibid., p. 180.

7. Amy Carmichael, *Edges of His Ways* (Fort Washington, PA: Christian Literature Crusade), p. 194.

8. Gail MacDonald, *High Call, High Privilege* (Wheaton, IL: Tyndale, 1984).

9. Quoted in Tileston, p. 109.

10. *Merriam-Webster Collegiate Thesaurus*, 2001, Online.

11. Ruth Harms Calkin, *Our Daily Bread* (1 July 1994).

Scripture
Index

Old Testament

New Testament

Notes